The Nobody's Guide to Health and Wealth

OrangeBooks Publication

1st Floor, Rajhans Arcade, Mall Road, Kohka, Bhilai, Chhattisgarh 490020
Website: **www.orangebooks.in**

First Edition, 2025

ISBN: 978-93-7426-984-8

Simple habits that actually work for normal people

The Nobody's Guide to Health and Wealth

DHANESH VALAPPIL

OrangeBooks Publication
www.orangebooks.in

Contents

Introduction

I'm a Nobody—And That's Why This Book Works for You

Let's get this out of the way—I'm not a multimillionaire.

If you're looking for a book written by someone with a hundred-million-dollar net worth, a massive YouTube following, and a body straight out of a fitness magazine, this book isn't for you.

I'm just a regular guy who—by 45 (as of 2025)—has:

Built a decent corpus of wealth—my net worth is in the single-digit millions, nothing crazy.

Kept my biological age at 36, even though my actual age is 45.

Designed a simple, repeatable system where my health and wealth improve automatically—without feeling like a grind.

That's it. No magic hacks. No secret formulas. No "one weird trick" that will make you rich or shredded overnight.

If that sounds disappointing, I'll save you the time—this book isn't for you.

But if you're tired of overcomplicated advice, of fitness plans that fall apart after two weeks, of financial strategies that assume you have unlimited discipline…

Then keep reading.

Getting healthier and wealthier have a common thing: **the earlier you start, the better.**

The C.A.S.H. Framework – A System That Works in the Real World

Every success in health and wealth comes down to four principles:

- **C - Consistency Over Intensity** – Small, steady habits matter more than extreme efforts.
- **A - Automation & Systems, Not Willpower** – Set up habits that run on autopilot.
- **S - Small Wins Compound Over Time** – Tiny actions create massive results over years.
- **H - Holistic Approach** – Health and wealth should support, not compete with, each other.

Let's say you want to walk more.

- C = You walk 6,000 steps daily instead of 15,000 once a week
- A = You schedule post-meal walks right into your calendar
- S = You celebrate hitting 8,000 steps, even if you didn't hit 10,000
- H = You don't ruin your knees by overtraining—health supports wealth

"Discipline is great. Systems are better."

This book will show you how to make these four principles work for you so success becomes automatic.

Your Brain is Running the Show – Why Health and Wealth Start in Your Head

Most people think they fail because they lack willpower.

But here's the real villain (or secret weapon): brain chemistry.

Your neurotransmitters—think of them as your brain's decision-making signals—influence everything:

- Whether you stick to a new habit or quit after a week.
- Whether you save and invest or blow your paycheck on impulse purchases.
- Whether you eat for energy or reach for junk food when stressed.

"Your brain isn't sabotaging you. It's just running the program it knows."

Throughout this book, you'll see how your brain chemistry shapes your health and financial habits—and more importantly, how you can use it to your advantage instead of feeling like you're fighting against yourself.

Don't worry, though—this isn't some deep science lecture. Neurotransmitters aren't complicated. Once you understand how they work, you'll see why some habits stick effortlessly while others feel like a constant battle.

Daily Habits That Compound

This book is built around simple daily actions that create massive long-term change—because that's what actually works.

Here are a few:

- Walking 10,000 steps a day (boring, but life-changing).
- Eating around 30 grams of protein per meal (no overcomplicated meal plans needed).
- Investing consistently (no stock-picking, just sustainable wealth-building).
- Walking after meals (small action, big metabolic payoff).

Too simple, isn't it?

But here's the thing—simple is what works.

"The basics are what people try after everything else fails."

People fail because they chase hacks, shortcuts, and extremes—but the real winners? They master the boring basics and let compounding do the work.

What You Won't Find in This Book

This book is not about:

- A magical diet where carb intake "doesn't matter."

- A secret financial strategy to find the next multi-bagger stock that grows 5x or 10x in a couple of years.
- A hidden stock trading or crypto arbitrage hack.

To be honest, I don't even know those strategies.

I'm not here to sell you some revolutionary new system—I'm here to show you what actually works in the real world.

"If someone promises overnight success, they're probably selling you a flashlight with dead batteries."

What You Will Get From This Book

By the end of this book, you'll know how to:

- Build a fit, strong body without extreme diets or training.
- Manage insulin, metabolism, and energy efficiently.
- Grow wealth beyond just compounding and index funds.
- Use neurotransmitters to your advantage for better decision-making.
- Create a lifestyle where health and wealth work together, not against each other.

This isn't another self-help book full of motivation with no execution. It's a real-life system designed for people who want to:

- Be healthier and wealthier.
- Enjoy life without obsession.
- Have a body and bank account that work for them—not against them.

Let's get started—

One simple habit, one smarter decision, and one better day at a time.

Chapter 1
The Hard Way to Learn About Health & Wealth

I earned more than my father before I turned 19. And I wasted most of it.

(That's not a brag. That's where this story begins.)

At just **19 years old**, I landed a **full-time job as a software engineer**. Unlike many others still trying to figure things out, I was already on payroll—thanks to the software boom in India and my not-so-bad programming skills. It was a rare combination of **timing, luck, and competence**.

I was earning **more than my 50-year-old father**—and living in a **low-cost, tier-3 city**, where money stretched far. You'd think I was on a fast track to success.

I wasn't.

Like most people who stumble into money young, I had **no idea what to do with it**.

"A salary means nothing if your savings silently vanish."

Sure, I was saving nearly **50% of my salary**. But all of it went into the **only options I knew**—fixed deposits and recurring deposit schemes. It felt responsible...

until inflation showed up and **quietly ate through it all**.

And there was another silent mistake:

I thought only in **Indian Rupees**. I never once considered **building a USD-centric portfolio**, or at least diversifying currency exposure. Over time, I watched what happens when you save in a currency that steadily weakens against the U.S. dollar.

"A weak portfolio in a weak currency is a double hit."

Health? Same Story, Different Flavour.

I wasn't just financially misguided—I was also physically underwhelming. I was **skinny. Not lean. Not toned. Just... skinny.** My metabolism was so high that even my **parents looked worried**. Their only advice?

"Eat more rice."

So that's what I did. **More rice. More parathas. More curries.** Basically, a carb carnival.

"Good programming got me in. Poor planning kept me stuck."

Protein? Rare. Vegetables? Decorative. Nutrition? Not part of the conversation.

As for exercise—back then, **the gym felt like a luxury item**. No one I knew went. It wasn't even aspirational.

The closest thing to working out was **playing cricket**, which, let's be honest, mostly meant **standing around in the sun**.

Looking back, my approach to both health and wealth was identical: Copy what others are doing and hope for the best.

Japan. Singapore. Bigger Paychecks. Bigger Blunders.

In **2004**, I moved to **Japan**. Great experience. Decent salary. Expensive lifestyle. At the end of each month, my **savings hovered below 20%**.

And where did those savings go? Into **insurance-linked investments**.

Ever signed up for something because it sounded smart—only to later realize the seller was the only one who got rich? Yeah, me too.

From Japan, I moved to **Singapore** and joined a **multinational investment bank**. My income improved. For the first time, I had a bank balance that looked semi-impressive. So naturally, I did the most impressive thing possible: I **started trading Indian stocks**.

A **well-meaning relative** got me excited about **high-beta stocks**. "This one's a rocket! That one's a 10X!" And I bought the dream.

I pumped **30–40% of my monthly savings** into the market. It was 2007. Everything was green. Until 2008 showed up.

Markets tanked. Stocks crashed. I panicked. But instead of cutting my losses, I doubled down—**bottom-fishing stocks that were "too cheap to ignore."**

Including the notorious Anil Dhirubhai Ambani Group (ADAG) stocks, trading at absurd discounts to book value.

"Cheap stocks are cheap for a reason. Respect that reason."

Turns out, there was a reason: scandals, mismanagement, and financial erosion. I lost almost everything in those trades.

Meanwhile, another trend was booming in India: **buying land**. The idea was simple—**flip it fast, or hold it forever** if it doesn't sell.

So, I followed the crowd and bought **2–3 plots**.

And then... regulations changed. **Black money dried up. Transactions slowed to a crawl.** Agents claimed prices had 5X'd on paper. But go try selling it? Good luck.

"If everyone's buying it, that's not proof. That's a warning."

Stumbling into Fitness

Around this time, something surprisingly good started happening—**thanks to a friend** who nudged me into the gym.

Our apartment had a small gym. Three days a week, I started showing up. I had **zero clue** what I was doing.

"The gym taught me what the stock market didn't—consistency over chaos."

Push day? Pull day? Never heard of those. I just **used whatever machine was free**. My workouts were as random as my stock picks.

And yet, **it helped**. Slowly, my body began to change. I felt stronger. More confident. And thankfully, **I escaped injuries**, despite my clueless training style.

The Real Shift: 2016

Then came **2016**. I lost my job. Suddenly, I had time—**real time**—for the first time in years.

And instead of panicking, I leaned in.

I started reading.

- "How the human body works?"
- "What macros and micronutrients actually mean?"
- "How economies function?"
- "Why index funds make sense?"
- "What intrinsic value really is?"

Somewhere along the way, something changed in me.

"The biggest transformation wasn't financial. It was cognitive."

I started **thinking differently**. I began **asking questions**—not just to others, but to myself. And I kept asking them until **I was truly convinced**.

Confidence wasn't enough anymore. I needed **logic. Data. Structure.**

"Data made me calmer. Emotion made me poorer."

I questioned everything. And I didn't care if my questions seemed silly. I only moved forward when the answers made sense.

I Didn't Choose the Long-Term Life... It Chose Me.

In the past, every time I bought a stock, it was with the **dream of a 20% return in 2 months**. But it never worked out like that.

The price would drop. I'd panic. Then I'd convince myself I was now a "**long-term investor.**"

"I didn't plan to be a long-term investor. My failed short-term trades forced me to become one."

It was a cycle of denial disguised as strategy.

Do I Regret Any of This? Not At All.

Would my journey have been smoother without these mistakes? Probably.

Do I regret them? **Absolutely not.**

"No regrets—only upgrades."

I don't believe in sitting with regret. I moved on. I learned. And I try—actively—to **never repeat the same mistakes again**.

Why This Book Exists

Most of my stories—especially those **before 2016**—come from an **Indian context**. But don't let that distract you. You'll likely find **parallels in your own market or life**.

What you won't find in this book is the usual drama. I didn't lose millions. I didn't make millions. I didn't go from couch to cover model in six months.

"I didn't lose millions. I didn't make millions. But I learned lessons that could help you avoid some expensive detours."

This book isn't about **spectacular wins**. It's about **relatable struggles**, **clear mistakes**, and **sustainable solutions**—from one nobody to another.

And trust me, small changes work—because they worked for me.

But none of it truly clicked until I stumbled into the most boring superpower of all time...

Consistency.

Chapter 2
The Power of Small, Consistent Actions

What if I told you the best financial decision I ever made was… forgetting about it?

No market timing. No stock-picking wizardry. No obsessively tracking charts. Just a simple, **set-it-and-forget-it** approach that led to something shocking.

Let's rewind to **2006**, a time when the Indian stock market was on a **bull run**, and everyone, including yours truly, felt like a financial genius. Riding this wave of optimism, I decided to **start investing**. No fancy strategies—just a **boring mutual fund tracking India's large-cap stocks**.

Feeling particularly savvy, I set up a **standing instruction to invest ₹10,000 every single month**. No active buying and selling, no market timing, just **boring, automated investing**.

For a while, my fund was **outperforming everything**. Even **Uncle Buffett** would've been impressed. Naturally, I took full credit, convinced I had cracked the **secret to getting rich**.

And so began my ritual: checking my portfolio **every single day**. Like some kind of stock market addict, I refreshed my account, watched the numbers tick up, and mentally calculated how many years before I could retire and buy a private island.

Then 2008 happened.

The market crashed. My fund plummeted. And suddenly, I wasn't an investing genius anymore. Like any good beginner investor, I reacted the only way I knew how—I **stopped looking**.

For **years**.

I completely forgot about it. But you know who didn't? **My bank's standing instruction.** That thing was more disciplined than most people's gym resolutions. Month after month, it kept investing ₹10,000. And me? I had no idea.

Fast forward to **2021**. COVID had shaken the world, markets had crashed and then recovered, and I was doing a deep dive into my finances. That's when I stumbled upon this **forgotten investment**. Curious, I tried logging into my mutual fund account.

Password incorrect.

Tried again. No luck.

After a series of **"Forgot Password" requests**, some bureaucratic back-and-forth, and a growing sense of annoyance, I finally got access.

And that's when I had my **WTF moment**.

Despite all my **early obsession, panic, and eventual neglect**, this investment had quietly turned into a

monster. No fancy stock picks. No brilliant timing. Just **boring, consistent, automated investing**.

Now, let me be clear—this mutual fund wasn't even a **top performer**. It didn't beat the **NIFTY 50** (India's equivalent of the S&P 500). But that didn't matter. The real magic wasn't in choosing the best fund; it was in the fact that I **kept investing, no matter what**.

To put things in perspective:

- ₹10,000 per month invested consistently for **15 years**
- Assuming an **11.49%** annual return (1% less than NIFTY 50)
- Total amount by 2021? Around ₹4.8 million.

That's **₹4.8 million** sitting in an account I had completely forgotten about.

Now, I'm not suggesting you go out, **buy a random mutual fund, forget your password**, and hope for the best. But there's something to be said about the power of **automation** and **staying out of your own way**.

Because let's be honest—most people do the **opposite**:

- They **panic and stop investing** when the market drops.
- They try to **time the market** (and fail miserably).
- They get **bored with "slow money"** and jump into the latest **crypto-frenzy** or stock hype.

My **accidental success** wasn't about being smart. It was about **being consistent**.

And guess what? The same principle applies to health.

The Accidental Walking Habit

As I mentioned in the previous chapter, losing my job in **2016** led me to Hong Kong for good. And if you've ever been to Hong Kong, you know that walking isn't just something people do—it's practically a **competitive sport**. No one strolls. They **speed-walk** like they're on their way to sign a billion-dollar business deal.

At first, I had no choice but to keep up. But before I knew it, walking had become **my default mode of transportation**. If I needed to go somewhere, my first instinct wasn't *"Should I take a cab?"* but *"Can I just walk there?"* (Side note: **walking is free**, which is an underrated benefit, especially in an expensive city like Hong Kong.)

Years later, walking is just **part of my life**. I don't even think about it—it's automatic. Whether I'm in Hong Kong or anywhere else, I walk **every single day**, rain or shine.

Of course, I could have come up with plenty of excuses **not** to walk:

- The streets are too crowded!
- It's too hot!
- It's raining!

- What if I get lost and end up in Mainland China by accident?
- What if a pigeon targets me?
- What if I trip, and the whole city witnesses my downfall?

But none of that mattered. Because I had a secret weapon that made walking not just tolerable, but enjoyable—podcasts.

For **two years straight**, I walked **every single day** while listening to podcasts. And something interesting happened:

- My knowledge base exploded.
- My brain plasticity improved.
- I absorbed information faster and made better connections across different topics.

I wasn't just randomly consuming information—I was **compounding knowledge**, just like my investments.

What started as casual listening turned into an **intellectual goldmine**. I learned about:

- Financial freedom
- Global politics
- Biology and human physiology
- Psychology and neuroscience
- Strength training and fitness
- Philosophy, history, and free-thinking

- Even random things like quantum physics and the history of bread

And because I was constantly feeding my brain new information **while moving**, my **cognitive function improved massively**.

Think of your brain like a **city**. Every time you learn something new, you're building a **new road**. The more roads you build, the **faster traffic (your thinking) flows**. Walking while learning? That's like upgrading those roads into **highways**.

This is neuroplasticity in action.

- **Physical movement increases neuroplasticity** (your brain's ability to form new connections).
- Learning new information while in motion helps retention.
- The more connections your brain makes, the faster you think and problem-solve.

In simple terms, walking with podcasts for two years rewired my brain for faster, smarter thinking.

The Walking & Investing Parallel

Just like that accidental mutual fund, my walking habit worked not because I had a perfect plan—but because I showed up daily, without much thought.

No big goals. No dramatic sprints. Just quiet, boring consistency.

And that's exactly how you win at both health and wealth.

You don't need genius insights or monk-like discipline.
You just need tiny actions that are so simple, they're hard to quit.

Because whether it's your money or your mind, your long-term results are built by the things you repeat—**especially the things you don't even notice you're repeating**.

But here's the kicker:

Most people think they're being consistent…

Until they actually **track** it.

They think they're walking enough. Saving enough. Sleeping enough.

They're not.

Our brains are fantastic at *feeling* like we're doing the right things.

But unless you've got some kind of feedback loop—some system to show you the real picture—you're just guessing.

So before we build better habits, we need one powerful skill:

Awareness.

And the simplest way to build it?

Tracking.

Not obsessively. Not perfectly. Just enough to **know where you stand**.

That's what we'll talk about next.

Let's figure out what you're really doing—and what it's quietly doing to you.

Chapter 3
The Power of Tracking

(a.k.a. Knowing Where the Hell You Stand)

So now that we've seen how small actions compound… let's make sure you actually know what you're doing each day. Because guessing isn't a strategy.

Before you fix anything, you need to know what's broken.

Before you improve anything, you need to know where you're starting.

And before you feel bad about your progress… you need to check if you're actually making some.

That's why tracking—just plain old tracking—is one of the most powerful, underrated tools in health and wealth building.

It's not sexy. It's not exciting. But it works.

Like underwear. Not flashy, but you'd be in serious trouble without it.

Let's Start with Wealth

Back in 2006, I had a vague feeling I wasn't doing great financially.

I wasn't flying business class or bathing in dividends. I was just... surviving.

Then one random weekend, I sat down, opened Excel (yes, we used it back then), and listed everything I owned:

- A modest fixed deposit
- A couple of index funds
- A dusty old provident fund
- A mutual fund someone sold me while I was waiting for a haircut
- A piece of land (valued at today's market price)
- Money I had lent to a friend—with small interest
- Cash and bank balances

Then I listed what I owed:

- A term loan
- A home loan

And guess what?

I wasn't broke.

I wasn't flying first class, but I wasn't financially crashing either.

That was the day I stopped guessing and started knowing.

From then on, something strange—but predictable—happened:

My net worth started increasing.

Not because I found a magical investment or bought Bitcoin at $1.

Just because I started paying attention.

I was tracking. That's it.

When You Track Something, You Tend to Care About It

And when you care about something, you tend to improve it.

This is true in every area:

- Track your time → waste less of it.
- Track your expenses → save more.
- Track your habits → build consistency.
- Track your screen time → cry a little, then uninstall Instagram.

Tracking pulls things out of autopilot and into awareness.

That shift alone creates change.

Now Let's Talk Health

You might *think* you're eating 1,500 calories a day. But when you actually track it… surprise!

Here's what a "light eating" day might secretly include:

- **One samosa** with evening chai: ~260 calories
- **Milk tea** (sugar + full cream): ~180
- Half a pint of beer: ~140
- Peanuts or namkeen: 150–200
- Two ghee rotis: easily 300+
- Plus the "small bite" of dessert that you swear doesn't count

Suddenly your 1,500-calorie day is pushing 2,900—and you're wondering why the scale isn't moving.

The food isn't the problem.

The lack of awareness is.

But Isn't Tracking a Pain?

Let me guess—you're thinking: Tracking sounds boring. Maybe even neurotic. Do I look like the kind of guy who even weighs peanuts?" Not anymore.

You don't need to measure everything or live in MyFitnessPal.

Just use your voice.

Tell ChatGPT, Gemini or your favourite AI tool:

"I had 2 eggs, 1 dosa, 1 samosa, 1 milk tea today."

Or:

"Here's my net worth this month: FD ₹5L, Index ₹8L, Land ₹12L, Loans ₹10L."

Boom. Logged. No spreadsheets. No judgment.

And no confusion about where your money—or your belly fat—is going.

Track Your Workouts Too (Seriously)

Most people wing their workouts.

If you're doing the same 10kg curls every Monday since 2022… you're not working out. You're just lifting memories.

Instead, just say:

"Push workout today: 3x10 incline press @ 20kg, 3x10 overhead @ 15kg, dips."

Then ask:

"Compare it to last push day and tell me the improvement."

"Suggest a slightly harder workout based on this."

You'll instantly know if you're progressing or plateauing.

Even simple tracking = forward momentum.

You don't need a coach yelling at you.

You just need data—and a little ego protection when ChatGPT says you haven't decreased your weight in 3 weeks.

But Don't Go Full Psycho

Tracking helps, but overtracking? That's anxiety in a spreadsheet.

Let me be clear:

- Checking your portfolio every hour? Not helping.
- Weighing yourself every morning and evening? Not helpful.
- Counting steps from your sofa to the fridge? That's not cardio. That's comedy.

What You Should Not Track

(Trust me, don't.)

- **Stock prices every hour** – You're not day trading. You're just day panicking.
- **Weight after every meal** – Food weighs something. That's not fat. It's physics.
- **One-night stands** – No further comment.
- **Steps from bedroom to fridge** – You're not crossing the Himalayas.
- **Calories burned during sex** – Not the moment for analytics.
- **How others are doing** – You don't need that kind of stress in your life.

What You Should Track

Here's your starter pack:

Wealth:

- Assets: Fixed deposits, index/mutual funds, land, PF, money lent
- Liabilities: Home loan, term loan
- Net worth (monthly or quarterly)
- Monthly expenses
- SIPs and investments
- Emergency fund (yes, it matters)

Health:

- Macronutrients (protein especially)
- Daily steps
- Weekly weight average
- Waist size (monthly or quarterly)
- Workout log (AI or notebook—whatever works)
- DEXA scan (every 6–12 months)
- Blood test (annually)
- Sleep (optional but useful)

Final Word

Tracking won't instantly make you rich or ripped.

But **not tracking** guarantees you'll stay stuck.

You don't need fancy tools. You don't need to track everything.

You just need to start with one thing.

Track it.

Understand it.

Adjust as you go.

That's how momentum begins.

Just like good underwear, you won't always notice it. But the day you forget it—you'll know.

"Okay, I know what I'm doing (tracking)... but why do I keep sabotaging myself anyway?"

That's where neurotransmitters come in.

Chapter 4
Power of Neurotransmitters

(Or: How I Tricked My Brain into Going to the Gym—Without Lying to It)

Even when we track everything, we still slip. We skip workouts, eat nonsense, and make impulse buys. Why? Let's ask your brain.

Let me ask you something:

Ever found yourself daydreaming about a cold craft pale ale at 5:45 p.m. on a Thursday?

Or skipped your planned workout because India is playing Pakistan and it's one of those *eight-hour tension rollercoasters* where even your smartwatch is stressed?

Yeah, me too.

This chapter is not about shaming those moments—it's about understanding *why they happen*, and how to work around them using your brain's own chemistry. You don't need willpower. You need **a few clever cheats**.

Your Brain Is a Chemical Salesman

Neurotransmitters are like chemical salespeople in your brain. They're always pitching you something:

- "This will feel amazing."
- "That's too hard, let's not."
- "Buy it, you deserve it."
- "Don't go to the gym, you're tired."

And they're good at their job.

But once you understand their tricks, you can start *negotiating*—and sometimes, even turn the tables.

Cravings, Triggers & the Pale Ale Dilemma

Let's start with dopamine, the kingpin.

Dopamine doesn't care about results. It's obsessed with anticipation. The moment you think of a cold beer, that tiny rush you feel? That's dopamine saying, *"Let's go!"*

My personal weakness? Craft pale ales. Citrusy, cold, perfectly hoppy.

But I realized I wasn't addicted to the *alcohol*—I was addicted to the ritual. The bottle clink. The crack of the cap. The chill in the hand. The "I earned this" story.

So I hacked it.

Now, I pour zero beer or a citrusy soda into a nice glass. Light's low. Feet up. Ritual intact. Craving satisfied. Belly and sleep? Unharmed.

Same dopamine. Different outcome.

India vs Pakistan & The Case of the Vanishing Gym Plan

Another day, another match. India vs Pakistan is on, and suddenly, your scheduled workout seems like it can wait… forever.

That's not laziness. That's dopamine again, whispering, "This match is way more exciting than that treadmill."

You can't eliminate dopamine. But you *can redirect it*.

Here's how I tricked myself:

During match breaks or even innings changeovers, I started doing **small movements**—walking around my condo, stretching, squats. Just 5 minutes.

That small "win" gave me a dopamine hit. And sometimes, while walking around, I'd *see the gym downstairs*.

And boom—**that visual cue** is what flipped the switch.

I'd think, "Maybe I'll just do 10 minutes."

Once I step in, 10 becomes 20. 20 becomes done.

No motivation. Just momentum.

Triggers, Cues & Cheating the System

Want to know a secret?

You don't need more discipline. You need better **cues**.

Visual cues. Location-based cues. Emotional cues. They're the spark that light up your brain's chemical dashboard.

Health Triggers

- Walking past your gym every day? That's a **dopamine + norepinephrine** opportunity.
- Seeing your running shoes by the door?
- Keeping healthy snacks visible, not buried behind the birthday cake from 2021 in your fridge?

All these are cues that nudge neurotransmitters in your favor.

Wealth Triggers

- Keeping your net worth spreadsheet open on your desktop?
- Auto-notifications every week showing how much you invested?
- A calendar reminder to "review the budget in 3 minutes" on Friday?

Those are serotonin-producing cues—tiny signals that say, "Hey, you're in control."

Movement Is the Ultimate Mood Shortcut

Let's talk about walking.

No fancy workout. No HIIT. Just *walking*. It's a drugstore of neurotransmitters:

- **Dopamine** – from the rhythm and sense of progress
- **Serotonin** – especially if there's sunlight or greenery
- **Norepinephrine** – kicks in to boost energy and alertness

This is why your best ideas pop up mid-walk.

This is why *"I'll just go for 5 minutes"* is a cheat code—because the chemicals *want* you to keep going.

That's how I convince myself to go to the gym. Not by yelling "JUST DO IT" into a mirror. But by taking a walk, passing the gym, letting the cues and chemicals do their thing.

How Tracking Triggers Serotonin (and More)

Let's say you update your net worth tracker and notice your investments have grown—even a little.

Boom: Dopamine.

Then you realize you stuck to your savings plan for 3 months in a row.

Boom: Serotonin.

Then you feel more alert and energized, motivated to read that article about ETFs.

Boom: Norepinephrine.

All from a spreadsheet.

That's not boring. That's *brain-altering*.

Put Your Brain on Your Team

Here's what this all boils down to:

You don't need to fight your brain.

You just need to feed it better triggers.

Want to work out?

Walk past your gym. Put your clothes out. Start with 2 minutes.

Want to spend less?

Open your tracker. Set a low-budget alert. Get a weekly "You're on track" notification.

Want to stop craving junk?

Keep your rituals—just swap the inputs. Soda in a wine glass can feel fancier than a beer can.

Final Punchline

You're not lazy.

You're not weak.

You're not "bad at habits."

You're just running on a brain that was designed to **chase rewards** and **conserve energy**—because for most of human history, that's what helped us survive.

But now?

That same brain is surrounded by dopamine traps and instant gratification.

So if you've struggled to stick to good habits, it's not your fault.

It's your wiring.

The good news?

You can work *with* your brain—by feeding it the right cues, rituals, and rewards.

And one of the most powerful ways to do that?

Move.

Not because you're punishing yourself.

Not because you're chasing six-pack abs.

But because movement unlocks your chemistry.

In the next chapter, I'll show you why one of the simplest forms of movement—something as basic as a brisk walk—can transform not just your health, but your mood, your motivation, and your metabolic engine.

You don't need to crush your body to rewire your brain.

You just need to show up.

Slowly. Steadily. Repeatedly.

Let's explore the magic of Zone 2.

Chapter 5

The 9th Wonder of the World – Zone 2 Cardio

Ever done one of those eight-hour hikes or played a marathon cricket or football match on a Sunday?

You finish the day feeling like a hero.

Calories burned: through the roof.

Steps: in the tens of thousands.

Sweat: buckets.

You tell yourself, "This was epic—I must've lost at least two kilos today!"

But here's what usually happens next...

You're in fatigue mode for the next three days. Maybe even a full week.

You feel too tired to move, too sore to train, and your appetite skyrockets.

You start eating more than usual—sometimes even **more than you burned that day**.

Sound familiar?

All the gains you made get quietly reversed by the recovery binge.

These kinds of workouts aren't bad—they're fun and memorable. But let's face it:

They're not sustainable.

And sustainability is the first rule of C.A.S.H. – forget intensity, what matters is what you can do again tomorrow.

Unless you're a professional cricketer, a mountain guide, or have some sort of *unreal daily motivation* for intense physical adventure...

This is not a repeatable strategy.

Let me introduce you instead to the unsung hero of the fitness world. It doesn't have a six-pack. It doesn't scream. It doesn't punch you in the face with pain. And it doesn't make you crawl out of a gym half-dead with sweat dripping from places you didn't know could sweat.

It just quietly gets the job done. It doesn't rely on hype or heroic effort. It runs on autopilot—like any good system should.

It's called **Zone 2 Cardio**.

And yes, I'm calling it the **9th wonder of the world**, right after compounding—the 8th one, as Einstein allegedly said.

Why?

Because it's that powerful. That underrated. And that **sustainable**.

Wait, What Is Zone 2 Cardio?

Let's keep it super simple.

If you can walk fast, maybe feel a little breathless, **but still carry on a slightly awkward conversation**—you're in Zone 2.

If you can sing your favorite Bollywood or Coldplay song while doing it? You're not working hard enough.

If you can't even say "I need water" without gasping? You've gone too far, my friend.

Zone 2 is the sweet spot.

Your heart rate goes up, but not too much.

Your body starts burning fat as a fuel.

Your mitochondria—those tiny power plants in your cells—start throwing a party.

Why Zone 2 is So Damn Important

We've been brainwashed to believe that unless we're destroying ourselves at the gym, it doesn't count.

But guess what?

Most of the magic actually happens in the boring stuff.

Zone 2 helps:

- **Build your mitochondrial capacity** (translation: your cells get better at producing energy)
- Improve your fat metabolism

- Lower your resting heart rate
- Enhance your recovery
- Boost your health span

Hold on—what's **health span**?

Let's clear this up.

Longevity = how long you live

Health span = how long you live *well*

Living to 95 in a hospital bed, on machines, with no energy, memory, or ability to wipe your own... nose? That's longevity.

But dancing at your granddaughter's wedding at 88 without a walker? That's health span.

Zone 2 cardio supports **health span**.

And that's what this book is all about. We're not trying to become Greek gods. We just want to be strong, mobile, and full of energy—**until the very end.**

And if you're curious how real people actually live like this, I highly recommend watching the **Netflix documentary on the Blue Zones**. It's not hype. It's people living long, active, happy lives without ever stepping into a gym.

My Zone 2 Cardio Journey

Let me tell you what I do. Nothing fancy. No Peloton. No overpriced memberships.

Most days:

- I hop on the **treadmill**, crank it to 5–6 km/h, slight incline, and walk for 45 minutes while listening to a podcast or watching random YouTube rabbit holes.
- I walk **outdoors** when the weather's good—no music, just observing trees and suspicious pigeons.
- Sometimes I do **indoor walking in circles** if I'm stuck at home or traveling.

Boring? Sure.

But I'm not training for the Olympics. I'm training to not fall apart.

And it works.

My heart rate improves. My resting pulse dropped. My DEXA scan looks better than it did **last year**—not five years ago.

That's the power of small, compounding actions. That's Zone 2.

Zone 2 Cardio Ideas You Can Start Today

- Brisk walking for 45–60 minutes
- Light cycling (outdoor or stationary)
- Hiking at a conversational pace
- Elliptical trainer at low resistance
- Jog-walk intervals (slow, gentle)
- Swimming (slow laps)

- Marching in place while binge-watching a series

No, you don't have to sprint or suffer. You just have to **show up regularly**.

Even **walking after each meal** counts—yep, that gentle 20-minute post-dinner stroll can be your mini Zone 2 session.

And if you want a number? Here it is:

150 minutes per week of Zone 2 Cardio. That's what **Dr. Andrew Huberman** and many experts recommend for optimal metabolic and cardiovascular benefits.

Break it into 30-minute chunks, five days a week. Or do 50 minutes, three times a week. Or even ten minutes after each meal, every day.

There's no perfect plan—just a **sustainable one**.

Don't Fall for the Sprinter Bias

You know those Olympic sprinters with bodies carved out of marble?

Let's be honest: they didn't get that way *because* they sprint. They sprint *because* they were born with those genetics.

That's called **confirmation bias**. We see the outcome and assume the cause. Don't fall for it.

Most of us are not built to be cheetahs. We're more like reliable donkeys.

And there's nothing wrong with being a donkey—just keep walking and you'll reach the mountain top.

The Zone 2 Secret in Blue Zones

Look at the Blue Zones—places like **Okinawa (Japan)** or **Sardinia (Italy)** where people live long, healthy lives.

Guess what's common?

They **walk up hills daily**. They do chores. They move around slowly and steadily. That's Zone 2 in disguise.

No CrossFit. No insane boot camps. Just **sustainable movement**.

They're not chasing aesthetics. They're chasing tomatoes up a hill and calling it lunch.

Again—**watch the Netflix documentary**. It'll change how you see daily movement.

What Zone 2 Cardio Teaches Us About Wealth

Here's the fun part: Zone 2 Cardio has a **wealth-building cousin**.

Think of it like this:

- HIIT = trading crypto during a bull run
- Zone 2 = investing in index funds and showing up for 30 years

Zone 2 is the dollar-cost averaging of your body.

Slow. Boring. Unsexy.

But devastatingly effective over time.

You don't need bursts of brilliance. You need **daily, consistent action** that compounds.

Just like in wealth, sustainability beats intensity.

You don't win because you did something dramatic. You win because you **didn't stop doing the simple thing**.

Closing Thought

If compounding is the 8th wonder of the world, Zone 2 Cardio is definitely the 9th.

It won't give you instant abs. But it will quietly sharpen your brain, strengthen your heart, fuel your mitochondria, and leave your doctor mildly confused by how young your vitals look.

It's the ultimate **C.A.S.H. habit**:

- Done with **Consistency**,
- Easily Automated,
- Full of Small Wins,
- And deeply **Holistic** for both mind and body.

So the next time someone asks,

"Why are you just walking on a treadmill for 45 minutes?"

Look them straight in the eye and say:

"I'm building mitochondria, baby. What are you doing?"

And here's the secret:

You don't need to do it at 5 a.m.

You don't need to cold plunge afterward.

You just need to show up—especially in the morning.

Because how you **start your day** often decides how everything else flows.

In the next chapter, I'll walk you through the ***exact*** **morning routine** I use to kickstart dopamine, clarity, and movement—without needing to become a monk.

Let's get into it.

Chapter 6
The Morning Routine

(a.k.a. How to Outsmart Your Groggy Brain Before It Outsmarts You)

Now that you know how powerful low-intensity movement is, let's talk about the best time to start using it—right when you wake up.

Let's get this out of the way right up front:

Yes, I'm heavily influenced by **Andrew Huberman** when it comes to morning routines.

But don't worry, this won't involve cold plunges, monk-like meditation, or waking up before Elon Musk.

This is about **realistic routines** that make you **feel better, think better, and live better**—especially if you do them consistently.

Now, you might be wondering:

"Sure, this sounds healthy. But how does it help with wealth building?"

Excellent question.

Because if you're going to build long-term wealth, you need three things working in your favor almost every day:

Good decisions. Good focus. Good energy.

A solid morning routine sets that up.

It supports your **neurotransmitters**, stabilizes your **mood**, enhances your **cognitive performance**, and avoids the **mental clutter** that derails your decision-making.

Better choices. Better thinking. Fewer stupid mistakes.

That's how health and wealth connect before 9 a.m.

So let's break down what that looks like.

Your Morning Routine Starts the Night Before

You thought we'd start at sunrise?

Nope. Your morning actually begins **the night before**, when you decide what time to go to sleep.

I'm not going to pretend you can (or should) sleep at 10:30 p.m. sharp every night like some kind of bedtime ninja. But you should aim to sleep around the **same general time window**—say, between **10 p.m. and 11 p.m.**

It keeps your body clock (your circadian rhythm) steady. And that pays off big time the next day.

Don't swing from 9 p.m. one night to 2 a.m. the next unless you're trying to confuse your brain into thinking it's living in three time zones.

Wake Up at a Consistent Time (Use That Alarm!)

Your brain likes predictability.

If you wake up at wildly different times each day, you throw it into chaos.

In my case, I wake up around **6:45 a.m. to 7:15 a.m.** unless I'm traveling.

And yes, I use an alarm.

Not the soft "birdsong in a meadow" type.

Something **mildly irritating** that gives me a reason to leave the bed (and not throw my phone across the room).

Step One: Hydrate Like a Functioning Adult

The first thing your body wants in the morning isn't caffeine.

It's **water**. Plain, glorious, no-frills **water**.

Even mild dehydration affects alertness, focus, and dopamine production. That glass of water is your brain's real wake-up juice.

I won't force a specific amount on you. But don't overthink it—just get some water in your system before you do anything else. This wakes you up more gently and replenishes what you lost overnight.

And yes—do this before coffee.

Smile. Greet. Be Human.

This one's underrated.

Smile at people. Say good morning.

Even if you're grumpy and still waking up—just a small smile or friendly "morning" to someone in your home, on your walk, or at the coffee shop helps set a positive tone for the day.

It's simple. It's free. And it makes you (and others) feel good.

Delay the Caffeine Hit (Trust Me)

I love coffee. You probably do too.

But if you slam a double espresso the moment you open your eyes, you're doing your body a disservice.

Here's why:

Your **cortisol**—a natural stimulant—is already high when you wake up. Adding caffeine at this point can mess with your body's natural rhythms and lead to an afternoon crash.

So:

Wait 30 to 45 minutes after waking before your first cup.

Then go ahead and enjoy it.

Now for the inevitable question:

How Much Coffee Is Okay?

If you're a moderate coffee drinker, 2–3 cups a day is totally fine for most people.

But here's the thing:

Caffeine can stay in your system for 8–10 hours. That means even if you drink your last cup at 3 p.m., it might still be messing with your sleep at 11 p.m.

So I suggest a little **trial and error**. Test your own caffeine sensitivity and see what cut-off works best for you.

Personally? I don't drink coffee **after 11 a.m.**

That's what works for my brain and my sleep.

Get That Morning Sunlight (Your Brain Still Thinks It's 50,000 B.C.)

After you hydrate—and maybe while you're sipping that first coffee—**go outside** for at least **5 minutes** of sunlight.

This isn't just a feel-good wellness tip.

This is **evolution** at work.

Your brain has been trained over hundreds of thousands of years to sync its internal clock with the **rising sun**. Before alarms, before caffeine, before LED lights—we had **sunlight**. That was nature's original "start your day" signal.

It's how our ancestors aligned their energy, sleep, and alertness.

Morning light literally calibrates your internal clock.

Back in the day, people didn't fire up CNN or check Slack first thing. They walked out of their cave, stretched, maybe grunted, and let the sun hit their face.

Your brain?

It still remembers that.

So give it what it expects.

This tiny act—done daily—checks all four C.A.S.H. boxes: it's consistent, automatic, rewarding, and holistic.

Move Your Body (Even a Little Bit)

Move. Your. Body.

This doesn't have to be a full-blown HIIT session or 10,000 steps by breakfast.

A **15-minute walk**, a short mobility routine, or some basic bodyweight exercises will do the trick.

The goal is to get blood flowing and to wake up your **dopamine system**—the stuff that helps drive motivation, creativity, and mental energy.

Bonus: Some of my best ideas come while walking. There's something about forward motion in the real world that wakes up the brain in ways that screens never can.

Don't Skip Breakfast (Unless You Want To)

Let's talk about food.

If you eat breakfast (I personally don't, but I won't insist you skip it), here's the golden rule:

Go easy on the carbs.

A high-carb breakfast—like toast, cereal, or even a big fruit smoothie—might give you a temporary buzz. But it often leads to a **mid-morning energy crash** and leaves you feeling sluggish.

Instead, try a protein- and fat-based breakfast.

Think eggs, Greek yogurt, nuts, avocado, maybe some cottage cheese or a protein shake.

Why? Without diving into complex metabolism lectures:

- Protein and fat are **digested more slowly** than carbs.
- That slower metabolism keeps you **fuller longer**.
- It stabilizes your energy and blood sugar for the rest of the morning.

Simple rule:

Less bread, more eggs.

(And if you can skip breakfast without turning into a hangry maniac—go for it.)

Delay the Smartphone Madness

Now, the hardest part:

Don't check your phone immediately.

Let me confess:

I struggle with this too.

And I really mean it.

But I've had phases where I deliberately avoided touching my phone—especially emails and social media—for **60 to 90 minutes** after waking up.

And those days?

Way better.

More clarity. Less reactivity. Better energy. Fewer mental spirals about things I can't control.

When you start your day by reading about Donald Trump's latest tariff plan or some new chaos in Indian politics, you clutter your brain before it's even had a chance to wake up properly.

Give your mind some breathing room.

There's plenty of noise waiting for you later.

Try the 5-Minute Breathing Reset

One last suggestion that takes almost no time and can **transform your day**:

Do a **5-minute breathing exercise** after your walk or morning sunlight.

You don't need an app, subscription, or training.

Just go to YouTube and search: "Andrew Huberman 5-minute breathing exercise."

That's it.

If you can do that **every single day**, your nervous system, your stress levels, and your focus will all thank you.

In Summary: Your New Morning Routine

Here's your cheat sheet for better mornings:

1. **Sleep around the same time** each night (ideally 10–11 p.m.).
2. **Wake up consistently** (set an alarm that actually works).
3. Hydrate with plain water—before anything else.
4. **Smile and greet others**—a simple, powerful mood reset.
5. **Delay caffeine** by 30–45 minutes.
6. **Experiment with how much coffee works for you.** (Caffeine lasts 8–10 hours; I avoid it after 11 a.m.)
7. **Get 5+ minutes of morning sunlight**—your brain's ancient wake-up call.
8. **Move your body**—a short walk or light workout is enough.
9. **Eat a protein- and fat-based breakfast** if you eat breakfast (low-carb = more energy).
10. **Avoid your phone** for 60–90 minutes if possible.

11. Try the 5-minute breathing exercise—search it, do it, repeat.

This routine isn't extreme.

It's not complicated.

And you know what?

It works.

It may seem "too simple" to be powerful—but that's the beauty of it. And once your morning is calm, your food decisions, your steps, and even your finances start falling into place. That's **C.A.S.H. in motion**—Consistency, Automation, Small Wins, Holistic health.

You're not chasing discipline. You're just building systems that don't break.

Simple things often work.

And this routine is easy to **stick with for years**—which is the whole point.

And once your mornings become simple and stable, you start seeing complexity everywhere else.

Too many choices. Too many distractions. Too much stuff—physically, digitally, mentally.

So next, let's clean that up.

Let's explore how doing less—**owning less, juggling less, even tracking less**—can help you live more.

Chapter 7
The Power of Less

Kyojutsu — a Japanese martial arts concept about truth and illusion — isn't just for swordplay. We do it to ourselves daily.

Let me tell you a secret.

I once had the world's most "productive" looking office room.

Books stacked in corners. Two laptops. An extra screen—because hey, more screens = more output, right? Sticky notes on walls. Resistance bands under the chair. Fancy notebooks. That one book I kept meaning to finish. TV mounted on the wall. A few gadgets I bought during some tech sale frenzy.

Everything had its place. It was tidy.

But I wasn't.

Every time I sat down to work, I'd find myself flipping open that book "just for two minutes," or adjusting something, or checking a device. I wasn't being lazy—I was drowning in options.

Eventually, I did something radical:

I removed the extras.

Books I hadn't touched? Packed away.

TV? Unplugged.

Gadgets? Gone.

Desk? Reduced to just a laptop, notepad, and water.

And suddenly, my mind felt lighter.

Like a browser with fewer tabs open.

Kyojutsu: Seeing Through the Illusion

In Japanese martial arts, **Kyojutsu** refers to the interplay of *truth and illusion*. It teaches you to mislead, to avoid being misled, and—most importantly—to recognize illusion when it's wearing a "useful" disguise.

Now here's the twist:

We do this to ourselves all the time.

We surround ourselves with things that *feel* productive. A million tools, diets, stocks, subscriptions, and strategies.

But here's the truth:

Most of it is noise.

Minimalism is clarity. And clarity is power.

Clutter Isn't Just Physical. It's Financial.

I used to think I was building a smart portfolio.

What I was really building was chaos.

At one point, I had:

- Over 25 different individual stocks in India,
- Multiple **mutual funds**: large-cap, mid-cap, small-cap, IT sector, and a few others,
- **Bank accounts** across India, Singapore, and **two in Hong Kong**,
- Fixed deposits, gold ETFs, global ETFs, and yes—
- **Investment-linked insurance policies** (easily one of my biggest financial blunders).

Here's what I've learned the hard way:

Never, ever mix insurance with investment.

It sounds like a smart combo—but it's the worst of both worlds. You get poor coverage and mediocre returns. All locked behind fees and complexity.

Eventually, I had to clean house.

Now my investments are simple:

- In the **U.S.**: low-cost index ETFs like **VTI** (total stock market) and **BND** (bonds).
- In India: just a Nifty 50 or Sensex index fund.
- For **China**: one ETF like **Hang Seng** or **CSI 300**, and that's it.

No stress. No drama.

Just clarity, with compounding on my side.

If you can't clearly explain why you own something—and where it fits in your plan—you probably shouldn't own it.

My Health Routine: From Chaos to Clarity

I used to rotate between:

- Resistance training
- Hot yoga
- HIIT
- YouTube cardio
- Half-hearted jogging attempts

It looked balanced. But it was scattered.

Sustainable? Not even close.

Now?

I walk. I lift. I stretch. That's it.

No apps shouting at me. No program fatigue. Just consistent, boring, effective habits.

My Daily Diet: So Simple It's Almost Boring

After years of hopping between "cut carbs," "cut fat," "skip dinner," "skip breakfast," etc., I figured out what actually worked **for me**.

Here's my rhythm now:

- **Intermittent fasting**: I fast from **10 p.m. to 1 p.m.** the next day. This is a long-term habit now—not a short-term experiment.

- **Breakfast** (technically): Just **1–2 cups of black coffee**, zero calories. **Caffeine cut-off: 11 a.m.**, to protect sleep quality later.
- **Lunch** (main meal of the day): A full, satisfying plate with a mix of **carbs, protein, and fats**.
- **Evening snacks & chai?** Skipped. Instead, I go for **3 scoops of whey protein**, spaced out as needed.
- **Dinner** (goal: 8 p.m., reality: often 9–9:30 p.m.): **Protein-rich**, **low-carb**, and **healthy fats**. *Tip*: Less carbs at night = **better sleep** and digestion.

Simple. Repeatable. Not Instagram-worthy—but it works.

Even My Phone Got the Kyojutsu Treatment

I used to have over **130 apps**.

Finance apps, news apps, four meditation apps (never used), stock tickers, ten messaging tools… you name it.

Now? 15–20 apps max.

No buzz. No endless scrolling. No distraction loop.

Just function over fluff.

Let's Talk About You

- How many **mutual funds** do you have—and do you know *why*?

- Do you own **investment-linked insurance**? (If yes, time for a hard look.)
- How many **apps** are silently draining your focus?
- Are your workouts built for *you*—or for the algorithm that sold it to you?

Kyojutsu isn't just about deception in martial arts.

It's about recognizing the illusions we create for ourselves.

Productivity. Diversification. Balance.

Sometimes, they're just clutter wearing nice clothes.

Final Thought: Subtract to Multiply

Real growth often starts by removing the stuff that doesn't matter.

Not by doing more. But by doing less—better.

So here's a challenge for today:

What can you subtract... so your most important priorities can finally breathe?

Maybe it's an app.

Maybe it's a false urgency.

Maybe it's just noise pretending to be important.

Make that space.

And then – just walk.

Because sometimes, the best way to sort your thoughts…

is one step at a time.

Chapter 8

The Power of Walking – One Step at a Time, One Thought at a Time

No gym. No pressure. Just walk.

Let me ask you something.

When was the last time you just *walked*—no purpose, no phone, no rushing—just walked?

If you're like how I used to be, maybe it's been a while. We usually walk only when we "have to"—to get to the train station, to pick up groceries, or when we can't find a parking spot. But what if I told you walking—just simple, slow walking—can be one of the most powerful habits for your **health, wealth, and happiness**?

I'm not exaggerating. And no, I'm not talking about power walking in tight track pants or jogging while timing your heart rate. I'm talking about walking… in your old T-shirt, regular shorts, and maybe even a $10 pair of slippers. That's how I started.

Want to hear the full story?

It All Started with Boredom (Thank You, COVID)

During the COVID-19 days, like most people, I was just trying to survive the boredom. Gyms were closed, travel was paused, and life felt like a paused YouTube video. I had a beautiful park nearby, so one morning I just… walked.

I wasn't counting steps. I wasn't even thinking about fitness. I just needed to kill time. And for some reason, I kept doing it. The park was green, the birds were singing, and the fresh air felt nicer than sitting at home with the news running in the background.

No special clothes. No expensive gear. Just walking.

And here's the fun part—**after doing it for about three weeks**, without even realizing, it became a habit.

Isn't it strange how we get used to something just by doing it again and again?

By the Way… I'm Walking Right Now

Yes, really. As I'm writing this chapter, I'm walking. Not even kidding. If I complete both the chapter and my steps together, I might hit **8,000 steps and one full chapter**. Multitasking, great, isn't it?

Have you ever done something like that—walked while solving a problem or thinking about work? You'll be surprised how productive you can be.

Walking Made Me Happy (Even Without Music)

One of the first big changes I noticed? **Happiness.**

Even when it was hot, I felt happier when I walked. The green trees, the birds, the sunshine—it all made a difference. I was smiling for no reason.

Have you felt that before? That feeling of peace when you're just walking, especially in nature?

And then I realized—hello, **Vitamin D!** Walking outside meant getting sunlight, which gave me this important vitamin our bodies really need. It helps your bones, your immunity, your energy, even your mood.

So, walking = happiness + Vitamin D. Not bad, right?

Walking Gave Me Great Ideas

Here's something interesting.

On days when I walked without listening to music or podcasts, **my brain went wild** (in a good way).

So many ideas came to me—some for work, some for personal goals, even some funny ones. I didn't plan it. It just happened.

One of my best decisions—to increase my investment in the U.S. stock market—came during a quiet walk.

Have you ever had one of those "aha!" moments while walking? Try it. No distractions, just you and your thoughts. It's amazing what your brain throws at you when it's not busy scrolling Instagram.

Learning While Walking

Of course, there are days I don't want to be alone with my thoughts. On those days, I listen to a good podcast. One of my favorites is Andrew Huberman. His episodes are long—like 2 hours—but if I spread them over 2–3 walks, I can finish one easily.

Not a fan of him? No problem. Pick whoever you like. Use that time to learn something useful, interesting, or even just fun.

And guess what? Walking is also a great time to take **online meetings**—you know, the kind where you don't need to share your screen. I've taken so many Zoom or Teams calls while walking in the park. I felt more clear-headed, more confident, and honestly, more alive.

Have you ever observed that you are much more confident when you take a meeting by standing or walking, rather than sitting? I mean the online meetings, especially the ones where you're just talking. Try it out sometime—whether it's with a colleague, a client, or even your boss. You'll sound more energetic, more focused, and more in control.

Try it once and see if you agree.

Walking Builds Relationships Too

This one's underrated.

Walking isn't just for alone time. It's one of the best times to **bond**—with your partner, your kid, your pet, or even your colleague.

Think about it—when you walk with someone, there's no pressure. No eye contact needed, no fancy setup. Just walking and talking. It's more natural, more relaxed. You'll be surprised how deep some of the conversations can go.

Do you have someone you can walk with today?

Let's Talk Calories (Because Why Not?)

Okay, so let's get to the numbers.

If you walk **10,000 steps a day**, you burn around **250 to 300 calories**. That's like skipping one milk tea and a biscuit. Not huge, but over weeks and months, that adds up.

That's like burning off that extra samosa you didn't plan but couldn't resist. Sounds familiar?

And remember, we're talking about **casual walking** here—not brisk walking or hill climbs.

So if you do your morning walk (maybe 4,000 steps) and add a couple of phone calls while walking around your home or office, you'll easily cross 8,000–10,000 steps. Some days, I hit **14,000 or even 16,000**—but I never aimed for that. It just happened over time.

And yes, there are lazy days too. Sometimes I hit just 9,000. Or less. And that's totally fine.

Do you beat yourself up when you miss your targets? Please don't. You're not a machine.

Start Small, Grow Slowly

If you're walking just 2,000 steps now, don't aim for 15,000 tomorrow. Start with **4,000**. Then move to **6,000**. Slowly build up.

You'll naturally reach a point where your body feels active but not tired. That's your sweet spot. Just stick with that for a while.

Have you ever made a drastic change and then dropped it after two weeks? Yeah, me too. That's why small steps work better. Always.

No Place to Walk? No Problem

Some people say, "I have nowhere to walk."

Really? Not even a temple ground nearby? A church compound? A school playground? Maybe a big empty space near your neighborhood?

If you're in India and the roads feel too dangerous, I get it. Safety comes first. But try to find some open, safe area. There's always *some* spot. No excuses.

And hey, don't use a taxi or motorbike for short distances. If the shop is 1 km away, **just walk** (if the weather is okay).

Even light rain? Try walking in the drizzle—it's fun. Ever tried it? You should. But if it's super hot, then please be smart. Use sunscreen, stay hydrated, and wear a cap. Take care of yourself.

Walking = Thinking Time + Meditation

Some people love meditation. Sitting quietly, closing eyes, deep breathing.

Me? I find walking is my meditation.

If I'm upset, had an argument, or just feeling low—I go for a walk. All the negative thoughts show up. And that's good. That means my brain is telling me something.

Walking helps me process emotions, make decisions, and clear my head.

Do you run away from those thoughts? Try walking instead. You'll come back feeling better. Maybe not with answers right away, but at least with more peace.

Track It (But Keep It Simple)

Once you've been walking regularly for a week or so, try **tracking** your steps.

No need for a $600 Apple Watch. There are $50 smartwatches or even free step-counting apps on your phone. Accuracy doesn't matter much—a 10% error is okay.

It's not about numbers. It's about **consistency**.

And once you see your step count going up… trust me, it feels good. Like getting a green tick from your own brain.

Walking and Wealth (What's the Link?)

Let's be honest—walking won't double your investments. It won't give you secret stock tips either.

But it will make your brain sharper. It will give you ideas. It will reduce stress. And that, my friend, is a solid base for better decisions—whether in money, work, or life.

Oh, and it might help you skip a few taxi fares too.

One Final Suggestion

If you can, make walking your **first activity** of the day.

Wake up, drink water, and go for a short walk. Even 10–15 minutes is great. It sets the tone. You'll feel fresh, focused, and more in control of your day.

Try it tomorrow morning? Just once. Then you decide.

By the way, I clocked **8,000 steps** while writing this chapter.

Not bad, right?

So… ready to walk?

Just start. No rules, no pressure. One step at a time, one thought at a time.

And next, we'll go even deeper.

Because walking is just one example.

What happens when your whole life is filled with small, boring, repeatable wins?

Let's find out.

Chapter 9

The Power of Minimalism

Why Less Stuff = More Health, More Wealth, More Sanity

Do you...

- Open your fridge and still feel like you have "nothing to eat"?
- Own 50 workout t-shirts but wear the same three on rotation?
- Have 137 apps on your phone... and use maybe six?
- Keep jumping between meditation apps, hoping one of them will finally Zen you out?
- Spend more time organizing your productivity tools than actually doing the work?
- Keep a bookshelf full of "I'll read it someday" books—but never do?
- Constantly feel busy, but not necessarily effective?
- Have more than 20 stocks in your portfolio and can't even name what half of them do?

- Keep switching from one YouTube finance expert to another, each promising the "best strategy for 2025"?
- Follow 10 different fitness gurus, all telling you different things—resulting in you doing nothing?
- Subscribe to five health newsletters and still feel confused about what to eat?

If any of these sound like you—don't worry, you're not broken. You're just overwhelmed. And minimalism might be the answer you didn't know you needed.

When I travel, I rarely check in luggage. Most of the time, I just carry **a single hand baggage**, usually under 10 kilograms. That's it. Whether it's a 3-day trip or a week-long one, I've learned that I don't need more. A couple of versatile shirts, gym shorts, one pair of shoes, and the essentials—that's enough. It's not just about packing light. It's a reflection of how I approach almost everything in life: simple, intentional, and minimal.

I'm a Minimalist. But Not That Monk Guy.

Let's get this straight—I'm not saying you should wear the same grey shirt every day, eat boiled broccoli, or give up your phone.

I love good design. I appreciate quality. I'll gladly use a top-end product **if** it genuinely adds value. If you think the iPhone is a beautifully engineered tool and it helps you work better—great. That's minimalism too.

But buying every new iPhone "just because" is not.

Minimalism isn't about spending less—it's about choosing better, and owning less junk.

Minimalism in Diet: Keep It Clean, Not Complicated

You don't need 47 exotic ingredients or 8 mini-meals a day. Here's what works:

- **Protein**: Get 1.2x your body weight in kg as grams of protein. Daily.

Examples? Beef steak, grilled fish, eggs, cottage cheese, or whey protein.

Not lentils (unless you enjoy 2-hour digestion marathons).

- **Fats**: Think quality—olive oil, ghee, coconut oil (yes, your grandma was right).

Not those mystery oils in 99-rupee snacks.

- **Carbs**: Important, but not the hero of your plate. Get enough to support your energy.
- **Fiber**: Yep, the unsexy cousin of protein. But fiber keeps things *moving*.

Start your day backed up, and everything feels off. You know what I mean.

And let's not forget **micronutrients**. They're like backstage crew—no spotlight, but without them, the show collapses.

Key ones:

- Zinc
- Magnesium
- Vitamin D
- B-complex
- Creatine (yes, technically not a micronutrient—but deserves a spot here)

Here's a hack: Do a blood test. If your numbers are solid, you're probably getting enough macro and micro nutrients. If something's off—adjust. No need for supplement guessing games.

Minimalism in Workouts: 30–45 Minutes of Focus

Forget complex split routines that make you feel like you need a PhD in biomechanics.

Do this instead:

- **Option 1:** Full-body workouts every other day.
- **Option 2:** Simple push–pull–legs rotation.
- **Duration:** 30 to 45 minutes of *actual* training—not scrolling memes between sets.

And yes, ChatGPT can generate a simple plan for you. No excuses.

You don't need 12 types of equipment. Just consistency, focus, and enough load to challenge yourself.

Minimalism in Wealth: One ETF > 20 Half-Baked Ideas

Let's be honest—if you hold more than 20 stocks, two things are probably true:

1. You're replicating what a low-cost ETF already does.
2. You don't know what half your stocks actually do.

It's fine. Most people fall into this trap trying to "optimize." But more often than not, complexity just adds stress—not returns.

Ask yourself:

- Can I consolidate into fewer stocks per region?
- Should I just switch to a solid, low-fee ETF?
- Am I chasing noise or building wealth?

And another red flag: if you follow 10 different financial influencers and another 10 health gurus... trust me, your brain's running 15 background apps at once.

Too much advice leads to *zero* action.

Pick one or two trusted sources. Tune out the rest.

Minimalism in Tools: The Case for Old-School Finance Apps

One of the smartest minimalist decisions you can make? Use an **old-school, boring** portfolio management app.

Here's why:

- Fancy trading apps like Robinhood make it *too easy* to trade.
- They're built to nudge you into buying and selling.
- Every alert, notification, and "hot stock tip" creates FOMO.
- And frequent trading usually leads to **worse** returns—not better.

Instead, pick something *boring*. Something that makes it hard to place a trade. Something that doesn't send you daily dopamine pings.

"The more old-fashioned your app is, the fewer trades you'll make—and the better your portfolio might perform."

Simple interface. Low temptation. Better outcomes.

Minimalism with AI: One Bullet, Multiple Targets

Let me share a shift that changed everything for me.

I used to have a bunch of apps:

- One to track my workouts
- One for my weight and waist
- One for my investments
- Another one for my food log

Too many clicks. Too many logins. Too much friction.

Then came AI.

Now I just use **one tool** (in my case, ChatGPT—but it could be your favorite AI assistant). Here's how I do it:

- After each meal, I literally say out loud:

"Hey, I had chicken curry with one paratha and a vegetable salad."

That's it.

The AI figures out the calories, macros, and tracks it for me.

- I check my weight and waist size daily. I just say:

"April 4th—body weight is 79.4 kg, waist is 89.5 cm."

Logged.

- I create **dedicated prompts** for each category:
    - Food & macros
    - Body stats
    - Workouts
    - Portfolio updates

That's it. One app. Human language. Minimal taps. **Maximum tracking.**

Consider this: one "mother" app, powered by AI, can now do the job of 5–6 different trackers—better, faster, and in a language you naturally use.

Minimalist tracking = better data, less burnout.

Digital Minimalism: Your Mind's Clutter Closet

It's not just your wardrobe or portfolio that needs cleaning up—your **digital life** could use some decluttering too.

Between WhatsApp groups, Telegram channels, Slack pings, email newsletters, YouTube algorithms, and breaking news alerts... your attention is being torn to pieces.

Try this:

- Turn off *all* non-essential notifications.
- Uninstall apps you haven't used in 30 days.
- Check emails just once or twice a day—not every 7 minutes.
- Stick to one note-taking or productivity app. You don't need five.
- Unfollow people who don't make your life better.

"Your brain wasn't built to process 37 WhatsApp chats, 4 email inboxes, and 6 YouTube tabs. No wonder you're tired."

Less noise = more clarity.

Minimalism in Time & Commitments: Learn to Say No

One of the most powerful minimalist habits? **Protecting your time.**

If your calendar looks like a crime scene, maybe it's time to clean it up.

Say **no** to:

- Pointless work meetings
- "Catch-up" calls that drain energy
- Random coffee chats you don't want
- Social invites out of guilt
- Projects that aren't aligned with your real goals

"Trust me—most meetings you're in are useless. The world won't end if you skip them."

Fewer commitments = more focus. It's that simple.

Minimalism in Goals: Don't Chase Everything

Trying to lose fat, run a marathon, build a six-pack, read 50 books, triple your income, and become a real estate mogul—all in the same month?

Relax.

Choose **1–2 high-leverage goals**. Do them well. Then move on to the next.

"One clear goal beats ten fuzzy dreams."

This applies to your health, your finances, even your self-improvement. Focus is power.

Minimalism in Environment: Clean Space, Clear Mind

What's around you affects how you feel—and what you do.

- Clear your desk.
- Clean your kitchen.
- Keep healthy foods visible.
- Store junk where it's harder to access.
- Simplify your home screen.

"Your environment is either a launchpad—or a trapdoor."

Make it easy to win. Remove friction. Keep the good stuff front and center.

Final Word: Enough Is Enough

Minimalism is not about deprivation.

It's about subtraction with intention.

It's about getting rid of the noise so you can actually hear your own thoughts.

It's about cutting the clutter so your actions become clearer.

Whether it's your diet, your gym plan, your wardrobe, your stock portfolio, or your calendar—ask:

"What's actually helping me… and what's just taking up space?"

Because in both health and wealth, it's rarely about adding more.

It's about doing the right things—on repeat.

And here's something you might not have realised yet: the clutter you remove during the day doesn't just free up time and energy.

It also frees up your **sleep**.

A clearer schedule means fewer late-night scrolls.

Less stimulation means deeper rest.

Simpler habits mean your brain can finally switch off at night.

In the next chapter, we'll explore why sleep isn't just rest—it's your secret weapon for better health, better decisions, and a calmer mind.

Let's get you sleeping like someone who's finally made space for it.

Chapter 10

The Secret Weapon Everyone Ignores: Sleep

(Yes, even you probably do.)

Let's start with a confession.

Until a few years ago, my sleep pattern was a beautiful mess. I treated sleep like it was a **bank account**. Monday to Friday, I'd run my balance low—just scraping by with 5 or 6 hours. But weekends? I'd crash and "top up" with 9 or 10 hours like I was collecting cashback. I truly believed I could **repay the sleep debt** like I repay my credit card bill.

Spoiler: Sleep doesn't work that way.

Some nights I'd be in bed by 10 p.m., feeling like a productivity guru. Other nights? 12:30 a.m. with a movie or mindless scrolling. Wake-up times? Anywhere between 7 and 8:30 depending on my mood. When I traveled—especially for work—it was even worse. I've had nights where I saw 2 a.m. or even 3 a.m. before sleeping.

And for the longest time, I thought I was fine.

To make it worse, I believed that **not dreaming meant better sleep**. I assumed my brain was going into super-deep-rest mode. But no—dreams (REM sleep) are not the enemy. In fact, if you're not dreaming, there's a good chance something's off.

All this chaos showed up in my life:

- Brain fog and sluggish decision-making
- Constant fatigue even after a long sleep
- Puffy eyes and tired-looking skin
- Irritability and weird cravings
- Skipped workouts and low motivation
- Terrible financial decisions made on impulse

Sleep impacts **everything**. Your health. Your mood. Your metabolism. Your self-control. Even your money.

Let's break this down in a way everyone can understand.

12 Things Everyone Should Know About Sleep

(Especially if you want better health and better wealth.)

1. **Sleep is NOT a bank account.**

You can't "top up" on weekends to cover weekday deficits. It's not how biology works. Every night you skip proper sleep, your body and brain pay the price the very next day.

2. **Light is a big deal—especially from an evolutionary lens.**

Thousands of years ago, our ancestors didn't stare at phones at midnight. Light meant two things: **Go hunt** or **stay alert for danger**. That's how our brains evolved. Bright lights = daytime = stay awake.

So, if you're bathing in blue light from your phone or laptop at 11 p.m., your brain still thinks it's hunting time. No wonder you can't fall asleep.

3. **Your last dose of caffeine matters. A LOT.**

Here's my rule: No coffee after **11 a.m.**

Why? Because caffeine stays in your system for **8 to 10 hours** (sometimes even 12!). Even if you feel sleepy, it still messes with deep sleep.

So whether it's coffee, tea, energy drinks, or even dark chocolate—set a cut-off time. Experiment.

In my case, any caffeine post-11 a.m. = struggling to sleep at 10:30 p.m.

4. **Sleep-deprived brains make dumb decisions.**

When you're low on sleep, your prefrontal cortex (your logic center) checks out. That means you're more impulsive, emotional, and reactive. This shows up in health (binge eating) and wealth (impulse shopping, risky investments).

5. **Alcohol may help you sleep faster—but the quality drops.**

I used to enjoy a beer or two in the evenings. But when I cut alcohol out—especially at night—my sleep got way better. We'll talk more about alcohol in another chapter, but for now, just remember: **Less alcohol = better REM and deep sleep**.

6. **Take zinc and magnesium—but take them smartly.**

I take both daily, but I don't wait until bedtime. I take them in the afternoon or early evening. They help relax the nervous system and support better sleep. But they're not sleeping pills—habits matter more.

7. **Track your sleep like you track your steps.**

If you own a $50–$100 smartwatch (even a basic one), use it! Track your sleep quality—REM, deep sleep, wake-ups. This data can change your life.

Sleep isn't just about hours. It's about **quality**.

8. **Your sleep need is personal—find YOUR number.**

Some people feel amazing after 6.5 hours. Others need 8 or 9. Don't blindly copy the "8 hours for all" rule.

Try this: Experiment for a few weeks. Sleep for 6.5 hours. Then try 8. Then 9.

Ask yourself: How do I feel the next day?

More alert? Less cravings? Better focus? That's your sleep number.

9. **Dinner decisions affect your sleep.**

Heavy carbs, sugar, spicy food, or alcohol close to bedtime = trouble. Try to eat at least **2 hours before** you sleep. Keep dinner lighter.

Think protein, some healthy fat, maybe a bit of veggies—not a giant bowl of pasta or spicy butter chicken at 10 p.m.

10. REM sleep = brain reset.

REM sleep is when you **dream**, and it's crucial for memory consolidation and emotional balance. If you're not dreaming often, or if your REM is too short, your brain might not be resetting properly. That impacts creativity, focus, and learning.

11. Deep sleep = body repair.

This is when your body rebuilds muscles, releases growth hormone, and strengthens your immune system. Less deep sleep = more fatigue, slower recovery, and faster aging.

12. Consistency beats perfection.

Today, I sleep between **10:30–11 p.m.** every day, even if I'm not sleepy. I may twist and turn some nights—but I'm still in bed, reducing light, away from the screen.

My wake-up time is consistent too: **7:30 a.m.**, even on weekends. That habit alone changed my energy, my discipline, and yes—even my net worth.

Wait, How Does Sleep Affect Wealth?

By now, you probably get how sleep messes with your health. But you might be wondering,

"Okay… but how does this impact my bank account?"

Fair question.

Here's the thing: sleep-deprived brains make bad money decisions.

When your brain is foggy, tired, and low on willpower, you're more likely to:

- **Buy something dumb online** at midnight just because it was on flash sale. (Yes, that 8th phone case or massage gun.)
- **Say yes to a high-EMI purchase** that you absolutely don't need, just because you don't feel like thinking it through.
- **Order junk food** instead of cooking—burning money *and* health at the same time.
- **Delay important decisions** (like filing your taxes or reviewing your investment portfolio) because your brain feels too slow to deal with it.
- **Fall for a get-rich-quick scheme** because your impulse control is low and the dopamine feels good.
- **Forget to cancel a subscription** that's quietly draining your account every month.
- **Skip work or deliver poorly** at your job because you're sleep-deprived—affecting performance, promotions, and income.

All because you didn't sleep properly.

Sleep doesn't just recharge your body—it recharges your **judgment**. And when your judgment is off, your wallet pays the price.

Want to Improve Your Sleep? Do These:

1. Set a consistent bedtime and wake-up time—even on weekends.
2. Avoid caffeine at least 8–10 hours before bed.
3. Dim your lights and reduce screen time after 8 p.m.
4. Try an eye mask—it's $5 magic.
5. Take zinc and magnesium (afternoon/early evening).
6. Eat a lighter dinner. Avoid sugar, spice, and heavy meals.
7. Use a smartwatch to track your REM and deep sleep.
8. Don't aim for perfection. Aim for small wins.

Final Thought: Sleep is a Multiplier

Good sleep doesn't just make you feel rested. It **multiplies** everything else: your energy, your willpower, your workouts, your food choices, your productivity, your decision-making.

Most people ignore sleep because it looks passive. But it's actually **where all the transformation happens.**

And once you fix your sleep?

You'll wonder how you ever lived without it.

But here's the thing—

Just when you start sleeping well, something else often sneaks in to wreck it.

Late-night drinks.

"Social" habits that quietly undo all your hard-earned progress.

You think you're relaxing... but your body's paying the price while you sleep (or try to).

In the next chapter, we'll talk about one of the most overrated health and wealth killers out there—**alcohol**.

No lectures. No guilt trips.

Just a fresh, real look at what it's really costing you—and what to do instead.

Let's open that bottle.

(Just not the kind you're thinking of.)

Chapter 11
Alcohol – The Good-Looking Assassin

"Sir, what can I make for you tonight?" — Translation: How should I kill you, boss?

Let me start with a question.

When was the last time you drank—not because you wanted to, but because it felt expected?

To celebrate. To impress. To "relax." To be polite.

We've all been there.

Before writing this chapter, I made myself a small promise:

No alcohol for three months.

Not because I had a drinking problem—but because I didn't want to write about this topic while sipping a gin and soda.

Now it's been nearly four months.

And this is the final chapter I wrote for the book.

I wanted a clear mind for this one. And now I have it.

The Polite Assassin

Imagine this.

You walk into a beautiful bar. Mood lighting. Nice music.

A charming bartender smiles and says,

"Sir, what can I make for you tonight?"

Sounds classy, right?

But if there were subtitles under that smile, they'd read:

"Hello boss. I'm a gentle assassin. How would you like to be slowly destroyed—on the rocks or shaken with ice?"

Because alcohol is poison.

It may look stylish, come in fancy glasses, and be socially accepted—but your body doesn't care.

It's a toxin, and the moment you sip it, your system goes into damage-control mode.

And this assassin is thoughtful.

Gives you a full menu of options:

- "Shall I use whiskey today?"
- "Beer, chilled and bubbly?"
- "Toddy, nice and natural?"
- "Wine, good for the heart?"
- "Or a calorie-conscious gin and soda?"

Pick your poison. Literally.

The "Natural" Nonsense

Let's address the big myth:

"No no, I don't drink all that. Just toddy—it's natural!"

Or the global version:

"I only take red wine. Good for the heart, yaar."

Sorry to disappoint you, but "natural" doesn't mean "healthy."

Snake venom is natural. So is cyanide.

But you don't pour that over ice with lemon, right?

Yes, alcohol might have one or two tiny positive effects on some health markers.

But it causes ten other problems.

And the net impact? A big fat negative.

Whether it comes from a coconut tree or a French vineyard, it's still ethanol or methanol.

Your liver doesn't care if it's local or imported.

It just wants it out.

So, if someone tells you,

"One glass of wine a day keeps the doctor away,"

feel free to smile and say,

"That line was probably written by a wine company, not a doctor."

I'm Not Your Science Teacher

Now don't expect a biology lecture from me.

I'm not here to explain how ethanol breaks down or which hormone crashes after your drink.

If you're curious to know the full science—how alcohol affects your brain, liver, hormones, sleep, and decision-making—

go to YouTube.

Search **"Andrew Huberman alcohol"** or other expert talks.

Watch just one. You'll be shocked. You'll be enlightened.

And you'll wonder why you ever believed wine was a health drink.

How Did You Feel the Next Day?

Let me ask you:

How do you usually feel the morning after a few drinks?

- Fresh and sharp?
- Clear-headed and energetic?
- Ready to dominate the day?

Didn't think so.

Even when I was having just a couple of drinks a week, I noticed:

- Brain fog
- Slower thinking
- Emotional swings
- Random skin issues
- Poor sleep
- Bloating and acidity

And the funny thing? I thought this was normal.

I used to proudly say:

"I only drink socially. I take gin and soda, fewer calories."

But my body didn't care about the calorie count.

It cared that I was dumping a toxin into the system and calling it "relaxation."

The Wealth Killer

Let's talk money.

Alcohol doesn't just hit your liver. It quietly empties your wallet too.

1. You Spend Without Realizing

After a few drinks, you get generous.

"Don't worry bro, this round is on me!"

"Let's get one more!"

And before you know it, you've paid for half the bar.

Next morning, you're checking your bill like,

"Who even ordered that much?"

2. You Make Emotional Money Decisions

Alcohol doesn't make you smarter. It just makes you *feel* smarter.

You suddenly become a genius in the stock market.

- "Let's go big on this—it's a breakout!"
- "Market's dipping—sell it all!"
- "Nvidia is flying—buy more now!"

And that's how bad trades happen.

When you talk business after alcohol, you are vulnerable.

Scammers love that situation.

Your filters drop. Your trust rises.

That's when shady deals get signed and stupid decisions get made.

The Client Trap

Here's the sad truth.

Many times, I wasn't drinking for me.

I was drinking for **work**.

Client dinners. Sales bonding. Company parties.

I thought it was part of the job. Part of the relationship-building.

But guess what?

I was damaging my liver and draining my wallet… to help my company close a deal.

That's not strategy. That's self-harm disguised as networking.

So I'll ask you this:

Are you drinking for your own joy—or to keep someone else happy?

The Social Pressure Dilemma

Now here's where it gets tricky.

You say "no" to a drink.

Your friend says:

- "Come on, just one won't hurt."
- "Don't be boring."
- "We're celebrating!"
- "Wine is good for you, you know."

But let me ask you:

If alcohol is the only thing connecting you and this person… is that really a friendship worth keeping?

Try suggesting something else next time:

- A zero beer
- A nice curry and biryani dinner
- A chilled coffee hangout

- Or even a walk in the park with great conversation

If the person still wants to meet, you've got a real friend.

If not? Well… you got your answer.

What Happened After I Quit

No dramatic announcement. I just stopped.

And here's what changed:

- Clearer thinking
- Better digestion
- More emotional stability
- Improved sleep
- Glowing skin (no kidding)
- Saved a lot of money
- More meaningful conversations
- Less regret the next day

I still go out. Still meet friends. Still attend events.

But now, I go with:

- Zero beer
- Citrusy soda with ice
- Sparkling water with lemon
- And a sharp brain that remembers everything

Will I Ever Drink Again?

Maybe.

If I'm with someone really important and it's culturally awkward to say no, I may sip.

But that's the exception.

Most of the time, I've seen the benefits of saying "no thanks."

And I like this new version of myself more.

Not morally. Just **functionally better**.

Before You Order That Next Drink...

Ask yourself a few simple questions:

- Why am I drinking tonight?
- How do I want to feel tomorrow morning?
- Do I really enjoy this drink—or just the social comfort it brings?
- Is this helping my health or hurting it?
- Would this friend still want to meet me if I said no to alcohol?

Just reflect. That's all.

Final Cheers (Minus the Poison)

This chapter isn't about guilt.

It's about **awareness**.

You don't have to quit forever.

You don't have to post about it.

You just need to know what you're choosing.

So the next time that friendly bartender smiles and asks,

"Sir, what can I make for you tonight?"

Smile back and say,

"Just lime and soda, please. I'd like to be sharp tomorrow."

Chapter 12
The Dogma Trap

For most of my life, I carried invisible baggage — a set of *ready-made truths* that I never really questioned.

Some came from school textbooks, some from politics, some from religion, and some from my profession.

I once believed Israel was purely the villain, Palestine purely the victim.

I thought Marxism was the most humane system.

I followed rituals I couldn't explain.

In tech, I believed front-end work was inferior.

In money, I believed louder people knew better.

In health, I believed every trend I saw online.

All of these were dogmas — stagnant water that had stopped flowing long ago.

And in stagnant water, mosquitoes of arrogance, ignorance, and fear begin to breed.

A free mind, like a river, keeps moving. It cleans itself through flow.

What Dogmas Really Are

Dogmas are not just about religion. They are any beliefs that we accept without question — the ones that make us feel secure, but quietly limit us.

They sound harmless:

"This political side can never be wrong."

"Stocks are gambling."

"Real men don't do yoga."

"This news channel always tells the truth."

Dogmas comfort us because they give certainty. But certainty and growth rarely coexist.

To live freely, the mind must stay in motion — always asking, *why?* and *what if I'm wrong?*

Scientific Knowledge vs. Scientific Temperament

You can have scientific knowledge without scientific temperament.

Knowledge teaches you what to think; temperament teaches you how to think.

A person with true scientific temperament questions even their own assumptions. They look for data before opinions, change their view when evidence changes, and are not afraid to say, *"I don't know."*

That single phrase is often the beginning of all learning.

Scientific temperament is not about memorizing facts — it's about curiosity with discipline, logic with humility.

The Dogmas I Carried

In politics, I believed one ideology could fix the world.

Reality taught me that compassion and productivity must coexist.

In religion, I practiced rituals I didn't understand.

Now, I look for purpose, not prescriptions.

In my career, I once dismissed design as secondary.

Then I watched a simple UI redesign improve adoption more than any algorithm.

In finance, I equated intelligence with returns.

Later I realized patience is the real alpha.

In health, I followed diet dogmas until my own data — sleep, bloodwork, energy — proved otherwise.

Each shattered belief was a small rebirth.

The News Trap

Modern media doesn't sell information; it sells emotion.

Outrage, pride, fear — anything that keeps you scrolling.

Every channel or news site has an audience it caters to, and they serve opinions dressed as facts.

So if you really want to know the truth behind an event, you must go deeper.

Read multiple sources, especially those that disagree.

Look for raw data, not adjectives.

Ask yourself – who benefits if I believe this version?

When you start following opinions blindly, you stop being informed.

You start being programmed.

That's how dogma spreads fastest today – not through religion, but through algorithms.

Never outsource your thinking.

A free thinker listens, verifies, and concludes independently.

The Battle in Our Heads

No one is entirely free from bias.

Even I carry them.

Our brains – those 1.6 kilograms of jelly upstairs – love shortcuts.

They crave certainty more than truth.

That's why being a free thinker is a lifelong practice, not a one-time decision.

Every time you catch yourself reacting emotionally, pause and ask:

"Am I following data or dopamine?"

That small pause is where wisdom lives.

The Cost of Dogma

Dogmas always charge rent.

They make you miss opportunities because "that's not for me."

They strain relationships when you can't tolerate another view.

They damage health because you trust fads over evidence.

They drain wealth because you believe hype over data.

Every bias you remove is like deleting malware from your mind — you think faster, clearer, and kinder.

Training the Scientific Mind

Building a rational, curious mind is not complicated.

It's built through daily, small actions:

Ask "why?" three times before accepting any claim.

Track your own numbers — in health, wealth, or productivity.

Read something that challenges your views.

Celebrate when you change your mind — that's a sign of strength, not weakness.

And above all, avoid attaching your identity to any single label.

The moment you say, *"I'm this kind of person,"* your learning stops.

Free Thinking in Action

You see a supplement claiming 400% testosterone boost—instead of buying it, you check the studies.

You see a YouTube expert warning of a market crash—you check long-term data, see every crash eventually recovers, and decide to stay calm.

Your company adopts AI — instead of fearing it, you master it, and become more valuable than ever.

That's scientific temperament in action — curiosity instead of panic.

How It Ties Back to C.A.S.H.

Free thinking strengthens every part of the framework.

Consistency — you stay open and keep learning.

Automation — you build logical systems that override impulse.

Small Wins — every bias you shed is one victory closer to clarity.

Holistic Balance – health, wealth, and peace grow together when your mind flows freely.

Curiosity compounds faster than money.

The River Within

Imagine your beliefs as a river.

When it flows, it stays pure.

When it stops, it rots.

Mosquitoes of ego and misinformation breed in that stillness.

Ask yourself tonight:

Which belief of mine has never been questioned?

Which topic makes me defensive?

Which truth have I repeated without evidence?

The answers show where your mind has stopped flowing.

The Dogma-Free Advantage

When you remove dogma, everything improves.

In health, you stop chasing fads and start following your body's data.

In wealth, you stop reacting to noise and build systems that last decades.

In your career, you stop fearing change and start riding it.

Dogma makes you heavy.

Curiosity makes you lighter.

And light things move further.

Keep the River Flowing

The battle never ends.

Each time you outgrow one dogma, a new one quietly forms.

That's okay — awareness itself is progress.

Scientific temperament is not cold logic. It's warm curiosity.

It's not anti-faith. It's anti-blindness.

It's not about rebelling against everyone. It's about being honest with yourself.

Dogma is stagnant water.

Free thinking is a flowing river.

In the river, life thrives.

In stagnation, mosquitoes breed.

Your Challenge

From today, don't accept anything until you're truly convinced.

Ask questions.

Look at facts.

Study the data.

When it comes to your health, your wealth, or your career, let evidence guide you, not opinions.

Don't rush to believe.

Don't cling to comfort.

Be curious enough to challenge — and humble enough to change.

Because once your mind starts flowing freely, everything else follows.

Conclusion So, What Now?

You made it. All the way to the end.

No really—**thank you**. In a world where attention spans are shorter than an Instagram Reel, you chose to read a book that talks about walking, tracking, sleeping well, and saying no to random beer invites. That's pretty cool.

Let me guess what you're thinking:

"Wait… that's it? That's your big secret?"

Yup. That's it.

No 100-day biohacking bootcamp.

No "buy this magic supplement stack."

Just simple, boring, daily stuff.

Stuff that doesn't look powerful—until it quietly changes your life.

Here's the thing: **it all compounds**.

Just like interest on your savings.

Just like belly fat from weekend bingeing.

Just like energy from quality sleep, movement, and saying no to junk.

This book was never about turning you into some shredded productivity monk with a $100M portfolio.

It's about helping you feel a bit better.

Move a bit more.

Spend a bit wiser.

And live with a bit more clarity and control.

I'm not here to impress you.

I'm just a regular guy who got tired of drifting. I figured out a few things that worked for me. I shared them. And now, it's your turn.

Try them.

Tweak them.

Make them yours.

Some habits will feel natural. Others might not. That's okay. You don't need to follow my version. You have your own body, your own brain, your own chaos. Build your version. Write your own script.

Honestly, I hope you do.

Maybe one day you'll write your own book.

Or a blog. Or a note to your future self.

Doesn't matter. Just **own it**.

Because you don't need six-pack abs.

You don't need a Lambo.

You don't need to chase every trend that screams "optimize your life!"

You just need a few solid habits.

Done consistently,

automated where you can,

built on small wins,

and always pointing toward a life that's **balanced, peaceful, and real**.

Simple? Yes.

Easy? Not always.

Worth it? Absolutely.

So I'll leave you with this:

- What's the one habit you'll start tomorrow?
- What's a small win you're proud of today?
- And what's really stopping you from getting started?

Take what you liked.

Ignore what didn't click.

But do something with it.

If this book becomes just another thing you read and forget, then honestly—I've failed.

But if it nudges you even 1% toward a better, healthier, wealthier life…

Then we both win.

Cheers to that.

(Zero beer, of course.)

About Me – The *Nobody* Who Wrote This

I'm not a certified fitness coach.

I'm not a multi-millionaire investor.

I'm not here to tell you what to do with your life.

I'm just someone who messed up enough times… and finally started doing a few simple things consistently.

This book is a collection of those things.

I work in the world of AI and digital transformation. But outside of work, I'm constantly learning how to simplify—from my morning routines, to how I invest, to how I think about food, movement, and habits.

I don't use social media (as part of my minimalist lifestyle).

But if something in this book resonated with you—or if you have your own version of C.A.S.H. you'd like to share—I'd love to hear it.

You can reach me at:

✉ dhaneshb@gmail.com

🔗 linkedin.com/in/dhanesh-valappil-2a6aa934

If you're trying to build a healthier body and a more stable financial life—without going to extremes—I hope this book helped in some small way.

Because honestly, that's all I set out to do.

– Dhanesh Valappil

www.ingramcontent.com/pod-product-compliance
Lightning Source LLC
Chambersburg PA
CBHW031351230926
51848CB00002B/477
* 9 7 8 9 3 7 4 2 6 9 8 4 8 *